COURTHOUSE STEPS
Q · U · I · L · T

BY JUDY KNOECHEL

a Quilt in a Day® Publication

To my trio of treasured sisters: Pat, El, and Kathy

Published by Quilt in a Day®, Inc.
1955 Diamond Street,
San Marcos, CA 92069

Copyright © 1995 by Judy Knoechel

First Printing March 1995

ISBN 0-922705-46-1

Editor Eleanor Burns

TABLE OF CONTENTS

INTRODUCTION

After my first book, *Bird's Eye Quilt,* came out in February 1993, I rejoiced for only a short time before I realized there was a void in my life. I had planned my life around meeting editorial deadlines. I was used to the stress and frustration of sitting at the computer writing and rewriting until I met the Quilt in a Day standard of clear instructions. Suddenly it was over, my little book, pardon my pun, had flown the nest and I needed another idea to nurture and develop.

As I cast about for inspiration, my thoughts constantly returned to the Log Cabin quilt. It is my favorite quilt and has so many intriguing variations. There is the Diamond Log Cabin, the Pineapple, and the Courthouse Steps to list a few. Of these, the Courthouse Steps has never been featured as a Quilt in a Day publication. When I finally decided on the Courthouse Steps for my next book, I had no idea where my decision would take me.

My earliest experiments with Courthouse Steps looked very much like Log Cabin with its seven different colors and a light and dark side. But, the look of the quilt didn't intrigue me. Eleanor suggested it might be an excellent quilt for children and I wrote the instructions in three different versions and tested it with young students and their parents. It worked, the students were thrilled, but I still wasn't happy. I tried scrap versions and quilts with oversized center squares and quilts with thirteen colors to name only a few.

Finally I found a Courthouse Steps that pleased me. I built up strips of the same fabric on each of the four sides of the center square and created a different look for Courthouse Steps. I thought, "This is it, I have found my book." My test students liked my idea, but they also had new creative ideas to inspire me. Before I realized what was happening, I was enlarging on my idea of what a Courthouse Steps could look like. I began moving the lights and darks around, varying the number of colors needed, and placing them on different parts of the block. This created totally different looks. I finally settled on four variations.

My quest for the perfect Courthouse Steps is now done. I invite you to explore this book, let your creativity run wild and tell me what secrets you discover on your quest for the perfect Courthouse Steps quilt.

Antique Courthouse Steps Quilt from Eleanor Burns Collection

History

During the 1850's an innovative quilter designed the first Log Cabin quilt. It quickly gained in popularity among quilters who not only shared the pattern, but designed their own variations. Among these Log Cabin variations was the Courthouse Steps.

If the Log Cabin block represented the warmth and stability of hearth and home, the Courthouse Steps stood for country and democracy. For it was in the Courthouse that the laws governing the land were written. Here were kept the deeds to their property, and the records of their births, deaths, and marriages.

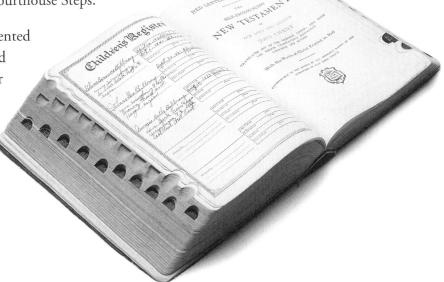

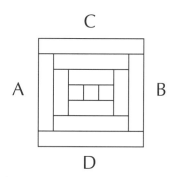

C

A | B

D

Look through the illustrations and photographs of the quilts. Note that there are four color variations of the Courthouse Steps block. Choose the one that you like. Each block variation has different layouts and they are not interchangeable.

CHOOSING A QUILT

Block 1

Five different fabrics are used to make the block. The Center Square is one fabric. Each of the other four fabrics are added to a side of the center square.

Block 2

Block 2 is a pair of Block 1 in mirror image.

Layout Choices for Block 1

- Windmill layout, pictured above
- Lanterns layout.

See page 9 for color photos of quilts.

Layout Choices for Block 2

- Mountains and Valleys layout
- Lanterns Barn Raising layout
- Chain Link layout, pictured above

See page 11 for color photos of quilts.

Selecting your Colors

Decide on several colors that work well together and show good contrast. Pick one multi-colored fabric that combines these colors. Incorporate this fabric into the quilt top or use it in the last border, and pull out colors that compliment it in the blocks. These colors should have different scales of prints and may read as solid when viewed from a distance. For all block variations, plan on using the center square fabric as the first border.

Blocks 1 and 2 Using two values of two colors works especially well for all layouts. The lantern layout also works well with four different colors as A, B, C, and D.

Blocks 3 and 4 Choose a white, ecru or light colored fabric that reads as solid for the background, B/D side, of the block. Avoid busy fabrics that distract from the overall design. If you are incorporating a multi-colored fabric, assign it to the C side of the block.

Block 3

Four different fabrics are used to make the block. The center square is one fabric. One fabric is used on two sides of the block. Two other fabrics are used on the remaining two sides.

Block 4

Block 4 is a pair of Block 3 in mirror image.

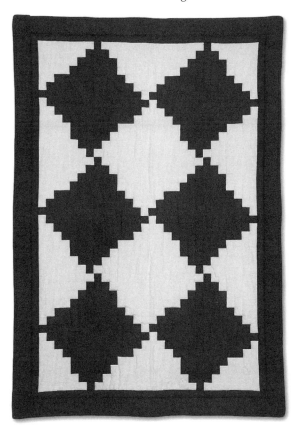

Layout Choices for Block 3

- Blossoms layout, pictured above
- Lanterns and Furrow layout

See page 13 for color photos of quilts.

Layout Choices for Block 4

- Lanterns Barn Raising with light or dark center
- Chevrons layout, pictured above
- Butterflies layout

See page 15 for color photos of quilts.

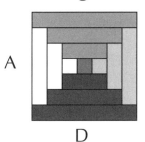

C

A   B

D

Block One

This is a five color variation of Courthouse Steps. The design is created by adding four contrasting colors to the four sides of the center square. A and C work together and B and D work together to create the design.

Yardage and Cutting Chart   Cut strips 2" wide selvage to selvage for blocks

	Center Square medium or dark	A Fabric light or medium	B Fabric light or medium	C Fabric medium or dark	D Fabric medium or dark
WALLHANGING 8 Blocks	⅛ yd cut 1 strip	⅜ yd cut 4 strips	⅜ yd cut 4 strips	½ yd cut 6 strips	½ yd cut 6 strips
BABY 16 Blocks	⅛ yd cut 1 strip	⅝ yd cut 7 strips	⅝ yd cut 7 strips	¾ yd cut 11 strips	¾ yd cut 11 strips
LAP ROBE 24 Blocks	¼ yd cut 2 strips	¾ yd cut 10 strips	¾ yd cut 10 strips	1⅛ yds cut 16 strips	1⅛ yds cut 16 strips
TWIN 32 Blocks	¼ yd cut 2 strips	1 yd cut 13 strips	1 yd cut 13 strips	1½ yds cut 22 strips	1½ yds cut 22 strips
DOUBLE 48 Blocks	⅓ yd cut 3 strips	1⅓ yds cut 19 strips	1⅓ yds cut 19 strips	2 yds cut 32 strips	2 yds cut 32 strips
QUEEN 48 Blocks	⅓ yd cut 3 strips	1⅓ yds cut 19 strips	1⅓ yds cut 19 strips	2 yds cut 32 strips	2 yds cut 32 strips
KING 64 Blocks	⅓ yd cut 4 strips	1⅝ yds cut 25 strips	1⅝ yds cut 25 strips	2⅝ yds cut 43 strips	2⅝ yds cut 43 strips

Borders and Finishing   Cut strips selvage to selvage

	1st Border same as center	2nd Border	3rd Border	Binding	Backing 44" wide fabric
WALLHANGING 30" x 51"	⅜ yd cut 4 2" wide strips	½ yd cut 4 3½" wide strips		½ yd cut 4 3" wide strips	1⅝ yds
BABY 52" x 52"	½ yd cut 5 2" wide strips	⅔ yd cut 5 4" wide strips		⅔ yd cut 6 3" wide strips	3¼ yds 2 equal pieces
LAP ROBE 53" x 74"	½ yd cut 6 2" wide strips	1 yd cut 6 4½" wide strips		⅔ yd cut 6 3" wide strips	4⅜ yds 2 equal pieces
TWIN 66" x 108"	⅞ yd cut 7 3½" wide strips	1¼ yds cut 8 4½" wide strips	1½ yds cut 9 5½" wide strips	1 yd cut 9 3" wide strips	6⅜ yds 2 equal pieces
DOUBLE 81" x 102"	1¼ yds cut 8 4½" wide strips	1⅝ yds cut 9 5½" wide strips		1 yd cut 10 3" wide strips	6¼ yds 2 equal pieces
QUEEN 87" x 108"	1 yd cut 8 3½" wide strips	1⅜ yds cut 9 4½" wide strips	1¾ yds cut 10 5½" wide strips	1 yd cut 10 3" wide strips	9½ yds 3 equal pieces
KING 108" x 108"	1 yd cut 9 3½" wide strips	1½ yds cut 10 4½" wide strips	1⅞ yds cut 11 5½" wide strips	1⅛ yds cut 11 3" wide strips	9¾ yds 3 equal pieces

Above Right

Baby quilt in Windmill layout. The purple and black windmills (B and D) make a strong color statement. The light green fabric (A) and the floral fabric (C) create one windmill in the center. Note the half-windmills around the edge of the quilt top.

Above Left

Lap quilt in Lantern layout. The multi-colored floral fabric (C), was chosen first. Corresponding jewel colored fabrics that read as solids were picked to complete the color arrangement. The green lantern is A. The smaller pink lantern is B and the larger purple lantern is D.

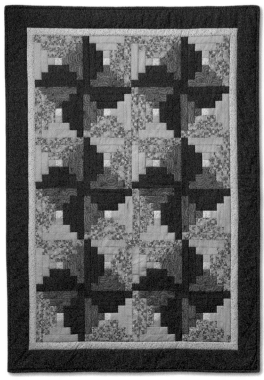

Lower Left

Lantern layout Baby quilt. Light and dark green lanterns (A and C) and light and dark purple lanterns (B and D) create a diagonal design across the quilt. The center square fabric repeats as the first border. The floral fabric repeats as the second border and binding. The quilt was stair-step quilted on the diagonal between the greens and purples.

Lower Right

Windmill quilt in lap size. Two values of purple (A and C) were chosen to be the dominant windmills. The soft green windmills (B and D) are in the center. When laying out your blocks, always arrange with both windmills in the dominant position to choose the better look. The quilt was stair-step quilted around the windmills.

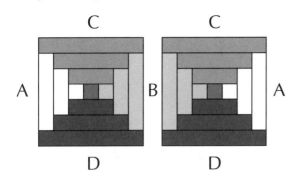

Block Two

This is a five color variation of Courthouse Steps in mirror image. The design is created by adding four contrasting colors to the four sides of the center square. A and C work together and B and D work together to create the design.

Yardage and Cutting Chart Cut strips 2" wide selvage to selvage for blocks

	Center Square medium or dark	A Fabric light or medium	B Fabric light or medium	C Fabric medium or dark	D Fabric medium or dark
BABY 16 Blocks	⅛ yd cut 1 strip	⅝ yd cut 7 strips	⅝ yd cut 7 strips	¾ yd cut 11 strips	¾ yd cut 11 strips
LAP ROBE 24 Blocks	¼ yd cut 2 strips	¾ yd cut 10 strips	¾ yd cut 10 strips	1⅛ yds cut 16 strips	1⅛ yds cut 16 strips
TWIN 32 Blocks	¼ yd cut 2 strips	1 yd cut 13 strips	1 yd cut 13 strips	1½ yds cut 22 strips	1½ yds cut 22 strips
DOUBLE 48 Blocks	⅓ yd cut 3 strips	1⅓ yds cut 19 strips	1⅓ yds cut 19 strips	2 yds cut 32 strips	2 yds cut 32 strips
QUEEN 48 Blocks	⅓ yd cut 3 strips	1⅓ yds cut 19 strips	1⅓ yds cut 19 strips	2 yds cut 32 strips	2 yds cut 32 strips
KING 64 Blocks	⅓ yd cut 4 strips	1⅝ yds cut 25 strips	1⅝ yds cut 25 strips	2⅝ yds cut 43 strips	2⅝ yds cut 43 strips

Yardage and Cutting Chart for Borders and Finishing Cut strips selvage to selvage

	1st Border same as center	2nd Border	3rd Border	Binding	Backing 44" wide fabric
BABY 52" x 52"	½ yd cut 5 2" wide strips	⅔ yd cut 5 4" wide strips		⅔ yd cut 6 3" wide strips	3¼ yds 2 equal pieces
LAP ROBE 53" x 74"	½ yd cut 6 2" wide strips	1 yd cut 6 4½" wide strips		⅔ yd cut 6 3" wide strips	4⅜ yds 2 equal pieces
TWIN 66" x 108"	⅞ yd cut 7 3½" wide strips	1¼ yds cut 8 4½" wide strips	1½ yds cut 9 5½" wide strips	1 yd cut 9 3" wide strips	6⅜ yds 2 equal pieces
DOUBLE 81" x 102"	1¼ yds cut 8 4½" wide strips	1⅝ yds cut 9 5½" wide strips		1 yd cut 10 3" wide strips	6¼ yds 2 equal pieces
QUEEN 87" x 108"	1 yd cut 8 3½" wide strips	1⅜ yds cut 9 4½" wide strips	1¾ yds cut 10 5½" wide strips	1 yd cut 10 3" wide strips	9½ yds 3 equal pieces
KING 108" x 108"	1 yd cut 9 3½" wide strips	1½ yds cut 10 4½" wide strips	1⅞ yds cut 11 5½" wide strips	1⅛ yds cut 11 3" wide strips	9¾ yds 3 equal pieces

Upper Left

Lap quilt in Mountains and Valleys layout. White and rose lanterns (A and D) and pink and floral lanterns (B and C) group together to form the mountains. The colors reverse at the top and pink and rose lanterns (B and D) flow downward alongside the white and floral lanterns (A and C) to form the valleys.

Upper Right

Lanterns Barn Raising Lap quilt. The light and dark blue lanterns (B and D) form the center diamond. The gold and floral lanterns (A and C) form the second diamond. They alternate to the edge of the quilt top.

Lower Left

Chain Link lap quilt. Light and dark pink lanterns (A and C) group together to make the "chain part" of the quilt. Burgundy and floral lanterns (B and D) repeat down the center and frame the chain at the edge of the quilt.

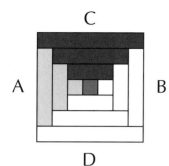

C

A   B

D

Block Three

This is a four color variation of Courthouse Steps. The design is created by A and C (the darks) lying side by side on the block, while B/D (the same light used twice) is diagonally opposite. The Center is medium.

Yardage and Cutting Chart Cut strips 2" wide selvage to selvage for blocks

	Center Square medium	A Fabric medium	B/D Fabric light	C Fabric dark
WALLHANGING 8 Blocks	⅛ yd cut 1 strip	⅜ yd cut 4 strips	¾ yd cut 10 strips	½ yd cut 6 strips
BABY 16 Blocks	⅛ yd cut 1 strip	⅝ yd cut 7 strips	1¼ yds cut 17 strips	¾ yd cut 11 strips
LAP ROBE 24 Blocks	¼ yd cut 2 strips	¾ yd cut 10 strips	1⅔ yds cut 26 strips	1⅛ yds cut 16 strips
TWIN 32 Blocks	¼ yd cut 2 strips	1 yd cut 13 strips	2¼ yds cut 35 strips	1½ yds cut 22 strips
DOUBLE 48 Blocks	⅓ yd cut 3 strips	1⅓ yds cut 19 strips	3⅛ yds cut 51 strips	2 yds cut 32 strips
QUEEN 48 Blocks	⅓ yd cut 3 strips	1⅓ yds cut 19 strips	3⅛ yds cut 51 strips	2 yds cut 32 strips
KING 64 Blocks	⅓ yd cut 4 strips	1⅝ yds cut 25 strips	4 yds cut 68 strips	2⅝ yds cut 43 strips

Yardage and Cutting Chart for Borders and Finishing Cut strips selvage to selvage

	1st Border same as center	2nd Border	3rd Border	Binding	Backing 44" wide fabric
WALLHANGING 30" x 51"	⅜ yd cut 4 2" wide strips	½ yd cut 4 3½" wide strips		½ yd cut 4 3" wide strips	1⅝ yds
BABY 52" x 52"	½ yd cut 5 2" wide strips	⅔ yd cut 5 4" wide strips		⅔ yd cut 6 3" wide strips	3¼ yds 2 equal pieces
LAP ROBE 53" x 74"	½ yd cut 6 2" wide strips	1 yd cut 6 4½" wide strips		⅔ yd cut 6 3" wide strips	4⅜ yds 2 equal pieces
TWIN 66" x 108"	⅞ yd cut 7 3½" wide strips	1¼ yds cut 8 4½" wide strips	1½ yds cut 9 5½" wide strips	1 yd cut 9 3" wide strips	6⅜ yds 2 equal pieces
DOUBLE 81" x 102"	1¼ yds cut 8 4½" wide strips	1⅝ yds cut 9 5½" wide strips		1 yd cut 10 3" wide strips	6¼ yds 2 equal pieces
QUEEN 87" x 108"	1 yd cut 8 3½" wide strips	1⅜ yds cut 9 4½" wide strips	1¾ yds cut 10 5½" wide strips	1 yd cut 10 3" wide strips	9½ yds 3 equal pieces
KING 108" x 108"	1 yd cut 9 3½" wide strips	1½ yds cut 10 4½" wide strips	1⅞ yds cut 11 5½" wide strips	1⅛ yds cut 11 3" wide strips	9¾ yds 3 equal pieces

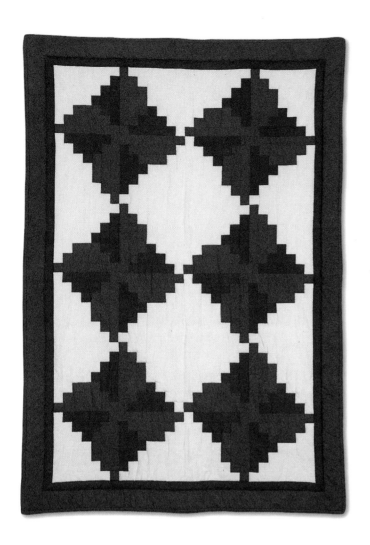

Upper Left

Lap quilt in Blossoms layout. Red and navy lanterns (A and C) stand out against an off-white background (B/D). The center square is also off-white. The navy fabric repeats as second border and binding.

Upper Right

Blossoms Wallhanging. A floral lantern (C) and peach lantern (A) make up the blossoms on an ecru background (B/D). The blue center square fabric repeats as the first border. This size wallhanging is ideal for narrow wall spaces. It is possible to follow the wallhanging yardage chart and make two four-block pillows.

Lower Right

Baby quilt in Lanterns and Furrow layout. The floral lantern (C) and peach lantern (A) create a diagonal design across the quilt alternating with an ecru (B/D) background. The same fabric was used in the wallhanging above. Arrange your blocks in both layouts to pick the arrangement you prefer.

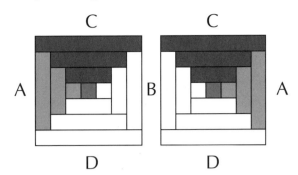

Block Four

This is a four color variation of Courthouse Steps in mirror image. The design is created by A and C (the darks) lying side by side on the block, while B/D (the same light used twice) is diagonally opposite. The center is medium.

Yardage and Cutting Chart Cut strips 2" wide selvage to selvage for blocks

	Center Square medium	A Fabric medium	B/D Fabric light	C Fabric dark
BABY 16 Blocks	⅛ yd cut 1 strip	⅝ yd cut 7 strips	1¼ yds cut 17 strips	¾ yd cut 11 strips
LAP ROBE 24 Blocks	¼ yd cut 2 strips	¾ yd cut 10 strips	1⅔ yds cut 26 strips	1⅛ yds cut 16 strips
TWIN 32 Blocks	¼ yd cut 2 strips	1 yd cut 13 strips	2¼ yds cut 35 strips	1½ yds cut 22 strips
DOUBLE 48 Blocks	⅓ yd cut 3 strips	1⅓ yds cut 19 strips	3⅛ yds cut 51 strips	2 yds cut 32 strips
QUEEN 48 Blocks	⅓ yd cut 3 strips	1⅓ yds cut 19 strips	3⅛ yds cut 51 strips	2 yds cut 32 strips
KING 64 Blocks	⅓ yd cut 4 strips	1⅝ yds cut 25 strips	4 yds cut 68 strips	2⅝ yds cut 43 strips

Yardage and Cutting Chart for Borders and Finishing Cut strips selvage to selvage

	1st Border same as center	2nd Border	3rd Border	Binding	Backing 44" wide fabric
BABY 52" x 52"	½ yd cut 5 2" wide strips	⅔ yd cut 5 4" wide strips		⅔ yd cut 6 3" wide strips	3¼ yds 2 equal pieces
LAP ROBE 53" x 74"	½ yd cut 6 2" wide strips	1 yd cut 6 4½" wide strips		⅔ yd cut 6 3" wide strips	4⅜ yds 2 equal pieces
TWIN 66" x 108"	⅞ yd cut 7 3½" wide strips	1¼ yds cut 8 4½" wide strips	1½ yds cut 9 5½" wide strips	1 yd cut 9 3" wide strips	6⅜ yds 2 equal pieces
DOUBLE 81" x 102"	1¼ yds cut 8 4½" wide strips	1⅝ yds cut 9 5½" wide strips		1 yd cut 10 3" wide strips	6¼ yds 2 equal pieces
QUEEN 87" x 108"	1 yd cut 8 3½" wide strips	1⅜ yds cut 9 4½" wide strips	1¾ yds cut 10 5½" wide strips	1 yd cut 10 3" wide strips	9½ yds 3 equal pieces
KING 108" x 108"	1 yd cut 9 3½" wide strips	1½ yds cut 10 4½" wide strips	1⅞ yds cut 11 5½" wide strips	1⅛ yds cut 11 3" wide strips	9¾ yds 3 equal pieces

Above Left

Chevrons layout in Lap quilt. Black floral lanterns (C) and peach lanterns (A) form the chevrons on a pale peach background (B/D). The green center square fabric repeats as the first border. The quilt is stairstep machine quilted "in the ditch" between the chevrons and background.

Lower Right

Lanterns Barn Raising with a dark center. The ecru fabric (B/D) frames the periwinkle (A) and floral (C) lanterns. Dark pink center is repeated in the first border. The quilt is stairstep quilted "in the ditch" between the diamonds.

Paste-Up Block

Paste up your sample block according to your block choice.

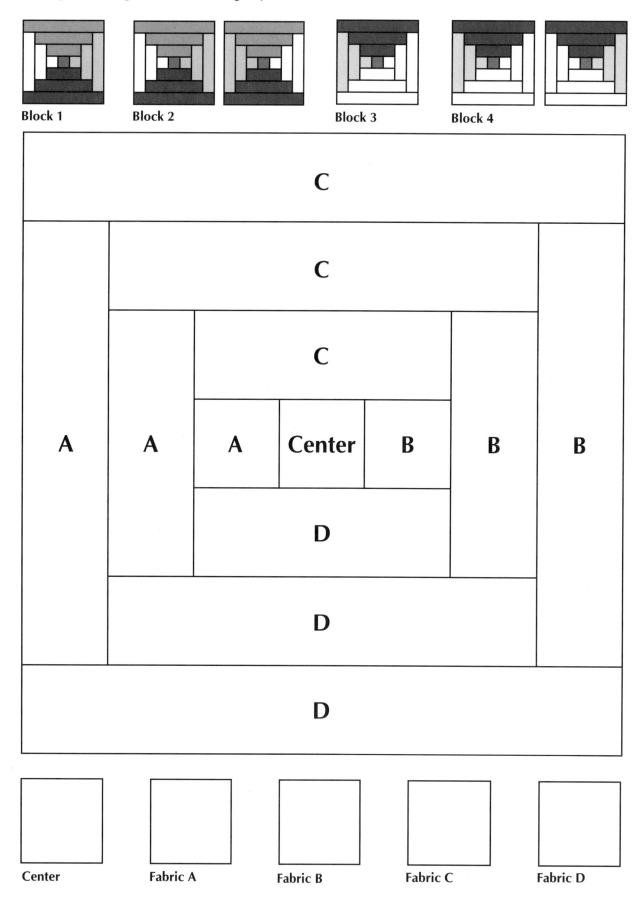

Block 1   **Block 2**   **Block 3**   **Block 4**

Center	
Fabric A	
Fabric B	
Fabric C	
Fabric D	

6" x 12" Ruler   6" x 24" Ruler   24" x 36" Cutting Mat

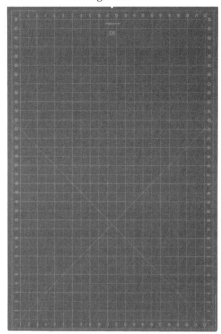

TECHNIQUES

Cutting

Use a large size rotary cutter with a sharp blade and a 6" x 24" plexiglass ruler on a gridded cutting mat.

Fiskars™
Rotary Cutter

1. Make a nick on the selvage edge, and tear your fabric from selvage to selvage to put the fabric on the straight of the grain.

2. Fold the fabric in half, matching the torn straight edge thread to thread.

3. With the fold of the fabric at the bottom, line up the torn edge of fabric on the gridded cutting mat with the left edge extended slightly to the left of zero. Reverse this procedure if you are left-handed.

4. Line up the 6" x 24" ruler on zero. Spread the fingers of your left hand to hold the ruler firmly. With the rotary cutter in your right hand, begin cutting with the blade off the fabric on the mat. Put all your strength into the rotary cutter as you cut away from you, and trim the torn, ragged edge.

5. Lift, and move the ruler over until it lines up with the desired strip width on the grid and cut. Accuracy is important. Strips for blocks are 2" wide. Border widths vary.

6. Open the first strip to see if it is straight. Check periodically. Make a straightening cut when necessary.

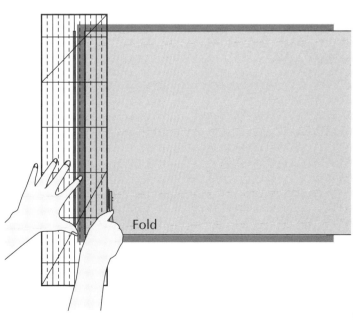

Fold

Sewing

Stitch size

Use a small stitch, 12 to 15 to the inch or a setting of 2.

¼" seam allowance

It is important to use a consistent seam allowance throughout the entire construction. Typically fabric is fed under the presser foot at its right edge. This isn't necessarily a ¼". Make a test sample and measure the seam allowance. If necessary, adjust the needle position, change the presser foot, or feed the fabric under the presser foot to achieve the ¼". A magnetic seam guide placed at the right of the presser foot will assure a consistent seam allowance.

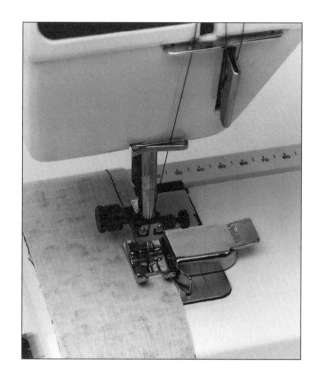

Serging

A person experienced with serging can construct the entire quilt top and borders with a serger. A five-thread serger is recommended.

Assembly-line sewing

This method saves time and thread by sewing blocks to a strip and butting on a new strip without cutting the thread until you are finished sewing. Use the stiletto to push wayward seams back in place.

Pressing

To "set and direct the seam allowance"

Throughout the construction, it is important to "set the seam" and then press the seam allowances in a given direction. Before opening, lay the sewn strips on the ironing board with a designated strip on the top. Lightly press the strip to "set the seam" as they lie right sides together.

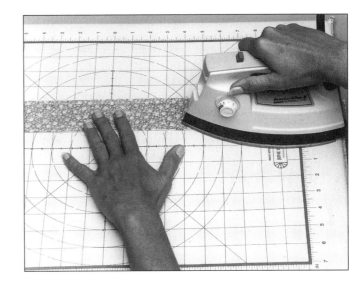

"Direct the Seam Allowance"

Lift the upper strip and press toward the fold. The seam will naturally fall behind the upper strip. Make sure there are no folds at the seam line.

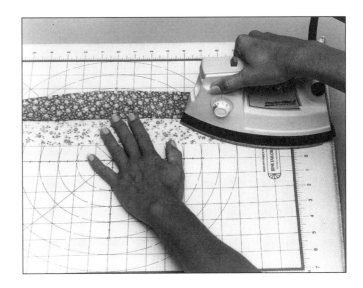

"Press Reverse Side"

Turn the strips over. Press the reverse side and check that the seams are pressed in the right direction.

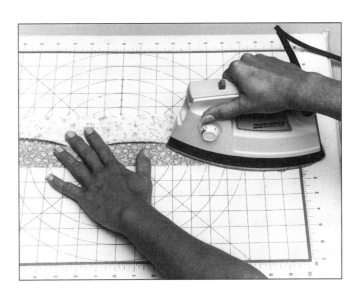

MAKING THE BLOCKS

Arranging Fabric Strips for All Blocks

Arrange 2" folded strips in the following order to the right of the sewing machine. Double check that the first border strips are removed from the stack of center strips.

Make five rectangular pieces of paper. Mark with Center, A, B, C, and D. Lay underneath appropriate stacks of strips.

A and C work together, and B and D work together to create the designs.

Refer to your Block Number throughout construction.

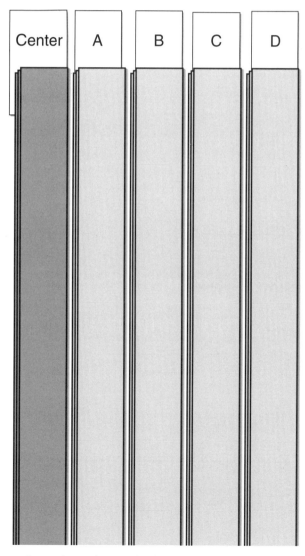

This is the order in which they will be used.

Sewing the Center

1. With strip A on top, put right sides together with Center strip. Sew the length of the strip.

Center

A

Use a ¼" seam allowance.
Use 12-15 stitches per inch,
or #2 on machine settings with 1-4.

Larger sizes repeat
until all Center strips are used.

2. Leave right sides together. Lay the closed strips on the ironing board with A on top. Lightly press the length of the strip to set the seam.

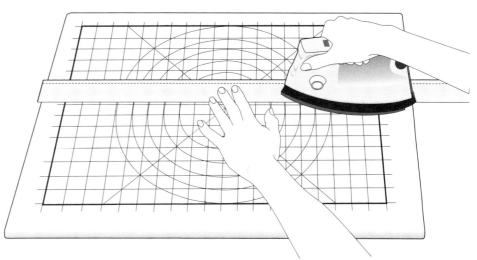

3. Lift the upper strip and press toward the fold, directing the seam allowance to fall behind A. Make sure there are no folds at the seam line. Turn the strip over and check that the seam is pressed in the correct direction.

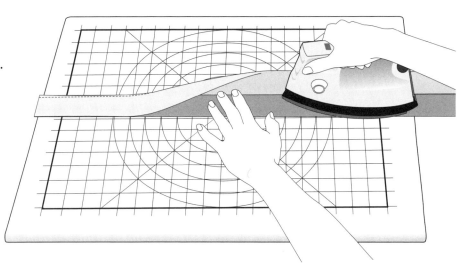

4. Sew B strip to the opposite side of the Center strip.

5. Lay the sewn strip on the ironing board with B on top. Set the seam, lift, and press.

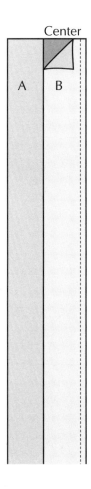

Center

A B

6. Lay the sewn strip on the gridded cutting mat, lining the bottom edge of the strip with a grid line. Square the left end to straighten and remove selvage.

7. Cut 2" wide blocks with a 6" x 12" ruler. Stack going in the same direction.

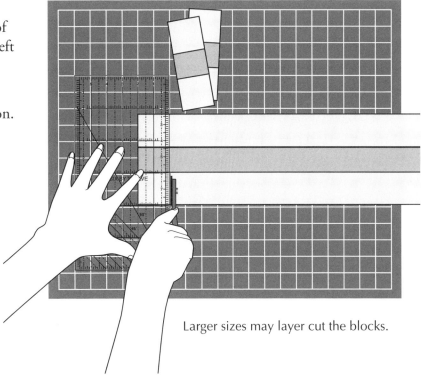

Larger sizes may layer cut the blocks.

Number of 2" wide blocks to cut

Wallhanging 8
Baby 16
Lap 24
Twin 32
Double 48
Queen 48
King 64

Adding the 1st C and D strip

1. Lay the 2" wide blocks right side down to the left of the sewing machine:

Blocks 1 and 3 only

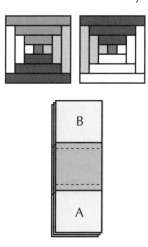

Arrange stack with B on top and A on the bottom. This placement is important to the future design layout choices, so double check that it is correct.

Blocks 2 …   and 4 only

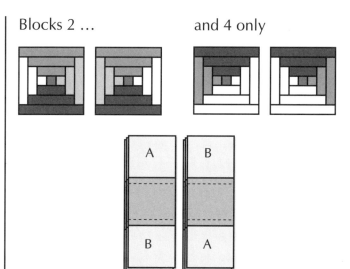

Divide 2" wide blocks into two equal stacks. Arrange one stack with B on top and A on bottom. Arrange second stack with A on top and B on bottom. This placement is important to the future design layout choices, so double check that it is correct.

Block 1 and 3

1. Lay a C strip right side up under the presser foot. Lay a block on the strip right side down.

2. Sew the length of the block. Stop when presser foot reaches the end of the block.

3. Butt the next block against it. Sew. Continue adding blocks to the strip. Start a new strip as needed.

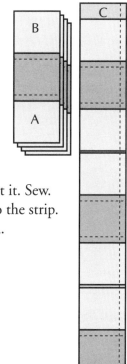

Block 2 and 4

1. Lay a C strip right side up under the presser foot. Lay a block on the strip right side down.

2. Sew the length of the block. Stop when presser foot reaches the end of the block.

3. Butt the next block against it. Sew. Continue adding blocks to the strip. Start a new strip as needed. Repeat for both stacks of blocks.

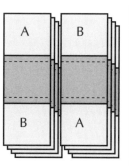

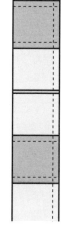

4. Lay the strip on the cutting mat with block side on top. Start at right end. Lay the ruler's horizontal line on the top of the block and the right edge of ruler along side of the block. Cut.

5. Repeat for all blocks.

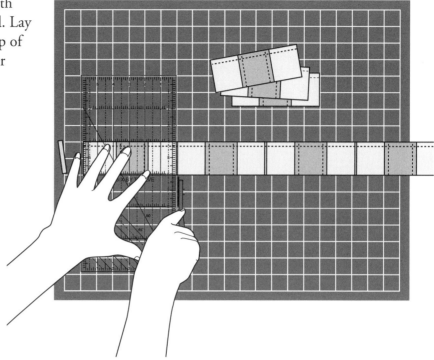

6. Check that blocks are trimmed straight at both ends.

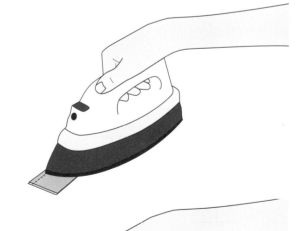

7. Turn stack over with C on top. Lay a block on the ironing board. Lightly press to set the seam.

8. Open and press, directing the seam allowance to C. Repeat for all blocks.

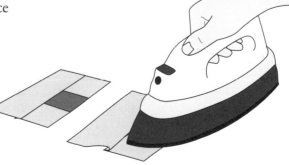

9. If necessary, trim edges.

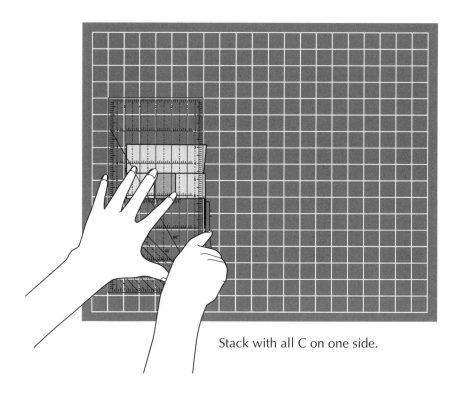

Stack with all C on one side.

10. Lay the blocks right side down to left of the sewing machine with C strip on the left. Lay a D strip right side up under the presser foot.

11. Lower the needle into the fabric to anchor it. Lay a block right side down on the strip. Sew. Add the next block. Repeat for all blocks, starting a new strip as needed.

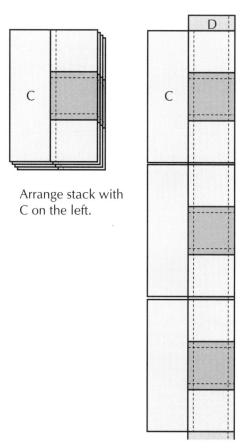

Arrange stack with C on the left.

12. Lay strip on the cutting mat with block side on top. Start at right side. Lay the ruler's horizontal line at bottom of block and the right edge of ruler along side of block. Cut. Check that blocks are trimmed straight at both ends. Turn stack over with D on top.

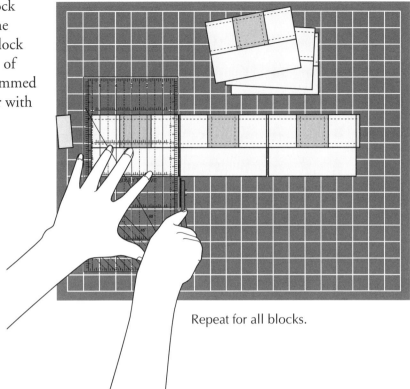

Repeat for all blocks.

13. Lay blocks on the ironing board with D strip on top. Set the seam. Open and press.

    There will be two stacks for Blocks 2 and 4. Put into one stack with A on one side, and B on the other.

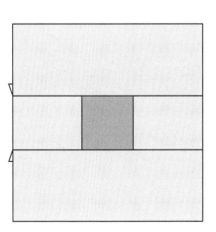

Adding the 2nd A and B

1. Lay the stack of blocks right side down to the left of the sewing machine. Arrange with A on the right and B on the left.

2. Lay strip A right side up under presser foot. Lay block right side down. Sew. Repeat for all blocks, adding new strips as needed.

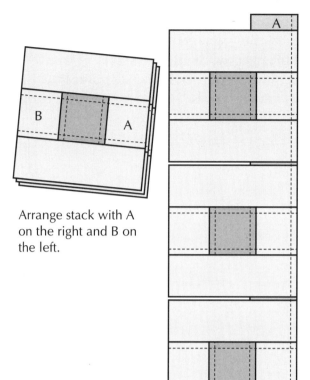

Arrange stack with A on the right and B on the left.

3. Flip all strips so the last block becomes the first block and the A strip is now on the left. Lay out a B strip.

4. Lay B strip right side up under presser foot. Lay first block on strip right side down. Sew.

   Repeat for all blocks on that strip.

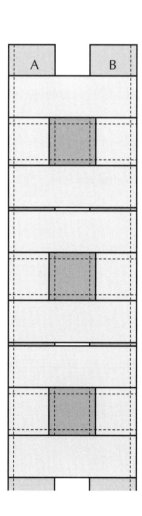

5. Lay closed strip on the cutting mat with block side on top. Start at right end. Lay the ruler's horizontal line on the stitching line at the top of the block, and the right edge of ruler along side of the block. Cut.

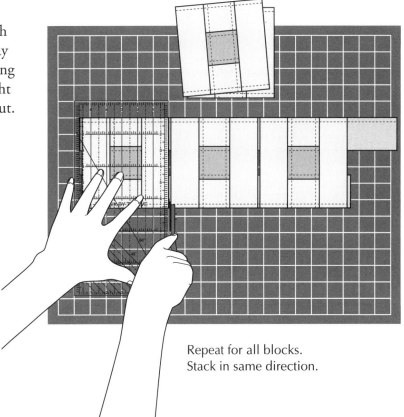

Repeat for all blocks.
Stack in same direction.

6. Lay closed block on ironing board with strip side on top. Lightly press to set the seams. Open and press both A and B. Stack in same direction.

There will be two stacks of Blocks 2 and 4. Put into one stack with C on one side, and D on the other.

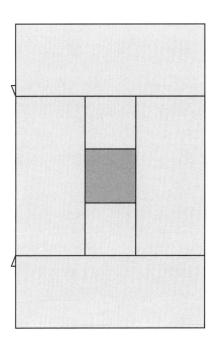

Adding the 2nd C and D

1. Lay the stack of blocks right side down to the left of the sewing machine. Arrange with C on the right and D on the left.

2. Lay C strip under presser foot. Sew all blocks.

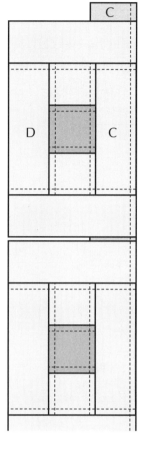

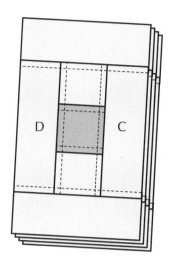

Arrange stack with C on the right and D on the left.

3. Flip blocks so C strip is on left. Add D strip.

4. Repeat cutting and pressing steps.

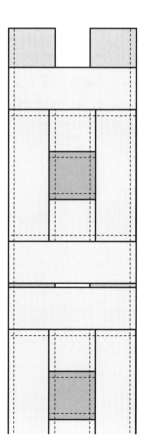

5. Add A and B strips to already established sides of block.

6. Repeat cutting and pressing steps.

7. Add C and D strips.

8. Repeat cutting and pressing steps. The blocks are complete when three strips are added beyond the Center square.

   After last pressing step, stack blocks 2 and 4 into two equal stacks.

Examples of the finished blocks.

Block 1   Block 3

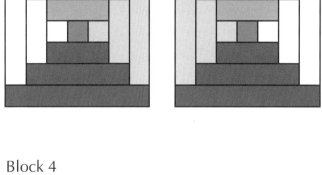

Block 2

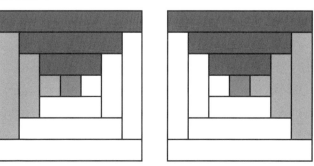

Block 4

LAYOUTS

Previewing the Quilt Top

1. Refer to the chart at the right for the layout choices for your block.

2. Arrange your blocks in rows in the various layouts. Pick your favorite.

3. Sew blocks together. See page 45.

Layout Choices for your Block	
Block 1 . . . . .page 33-34	
Block 2 . . . . .page 35-38	
Block 3 . . . . .page 39-40	
Block 4 . . . . .page 41-44	

Blocks Across & Down	
Wallhanging . . . . .2 x 4	
Baby . . . . .4 x 4	
Lap . . . . .4 x 6	
Twin . . . . .4 x 8	
Double . . . . .6 x 8	
Queen . . . . .6 x 8	
King . . . . .8 x 8	

Block 1

Lanterns Layout

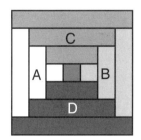

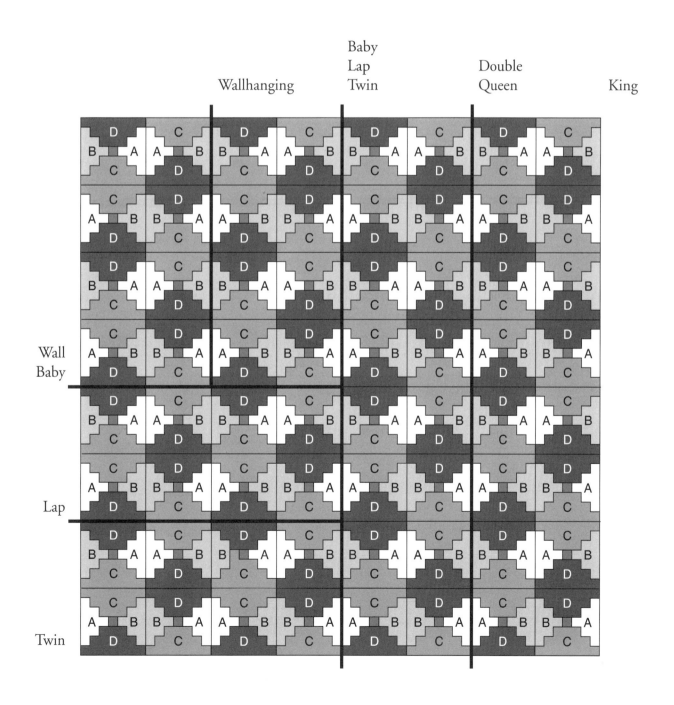

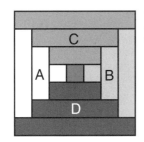

Block 1
Windmills Layout

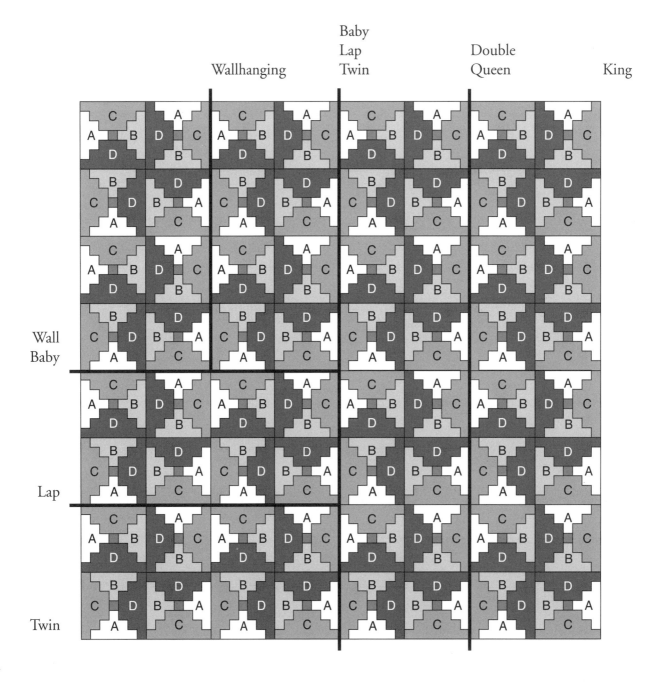

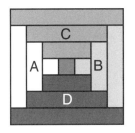
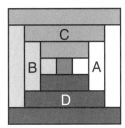

Block 2
Chain Link Layout

Start from center.

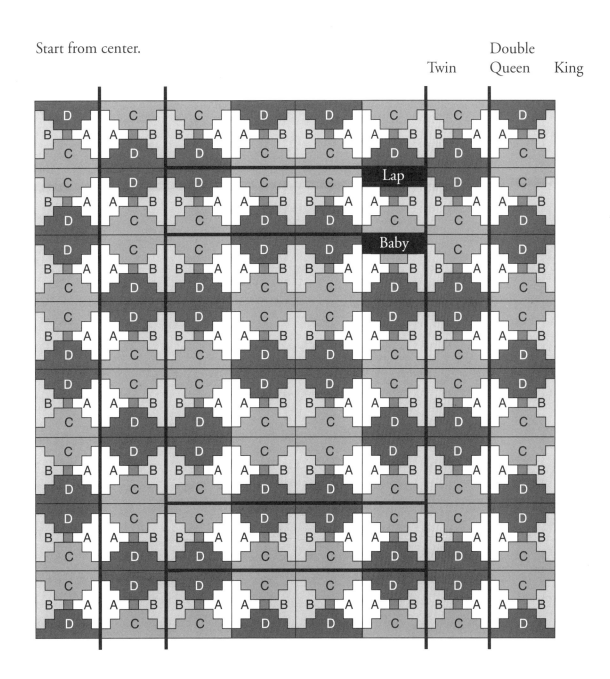

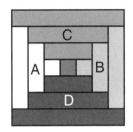 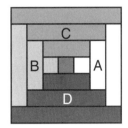

Block 2
Mountains and Valleys Layout

Start from center.

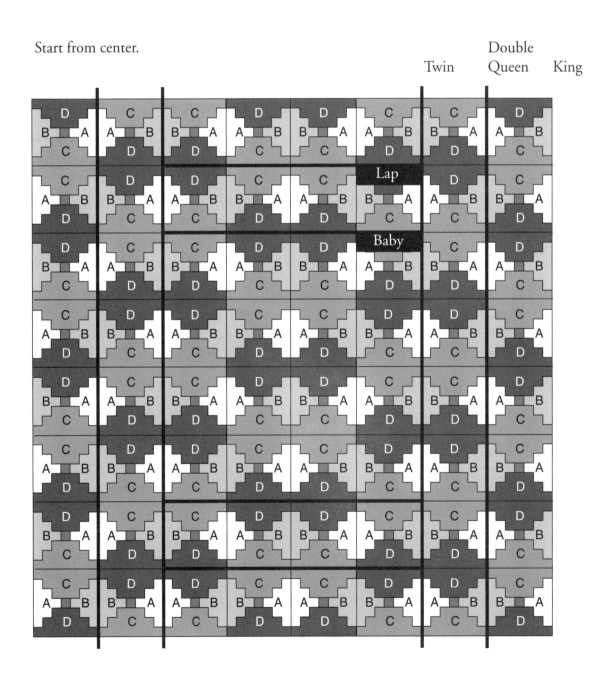

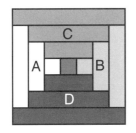 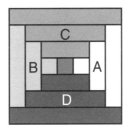

Block 2
Lanterns Barn Raising Layout with B and D Center

Start from center.

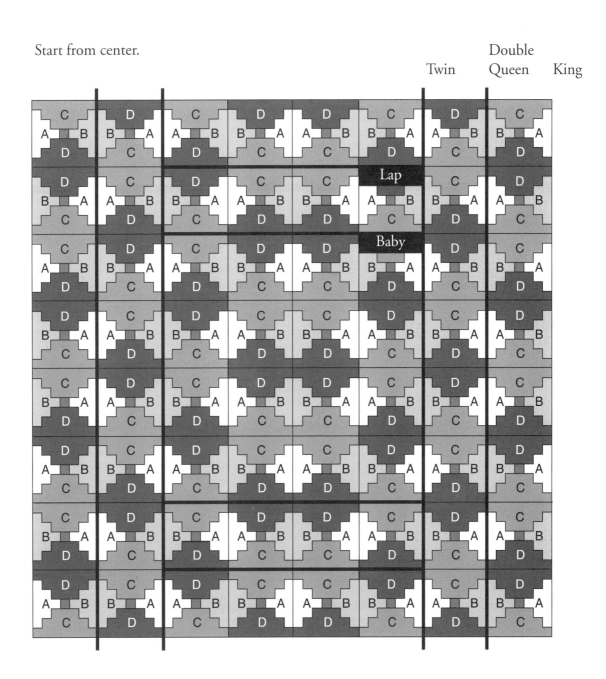

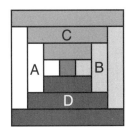 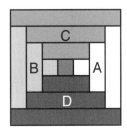

Block 2

Lanterns Barn Raising Layout with A and C Center

Start from center.

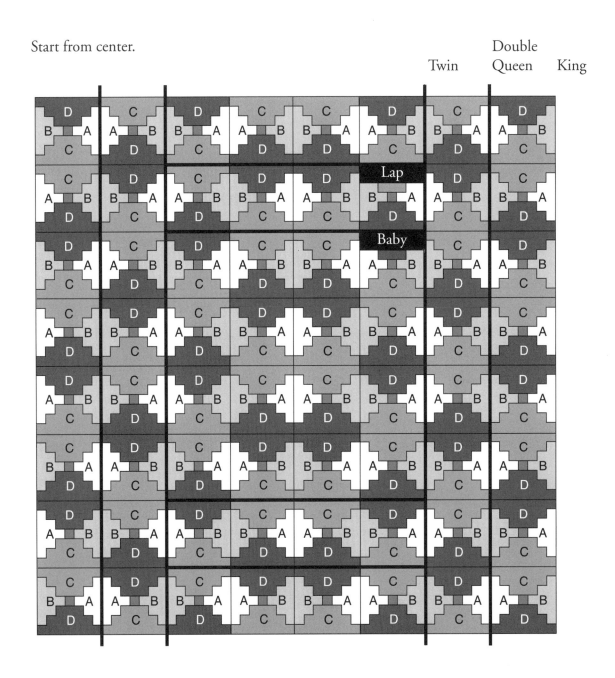

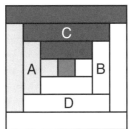

Block 3
Lanterns and Furrows Layout

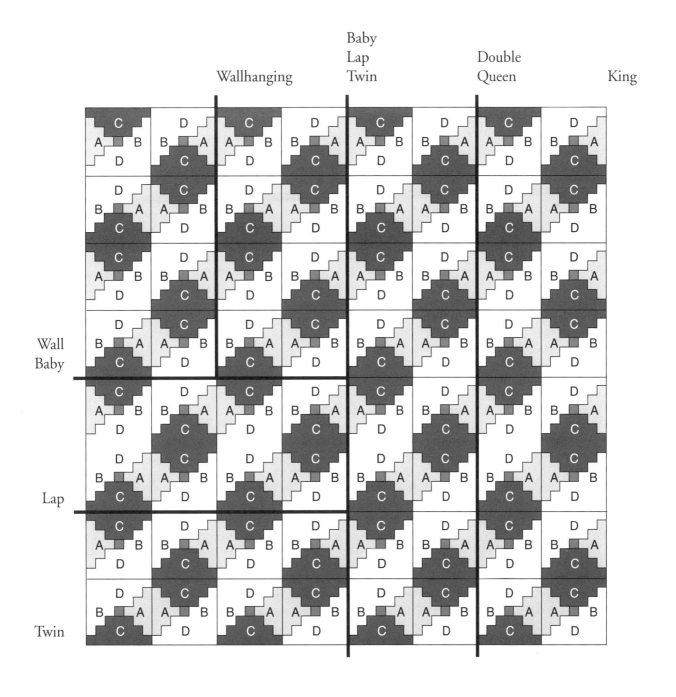

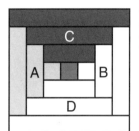

Block 3
Blossoms Layout

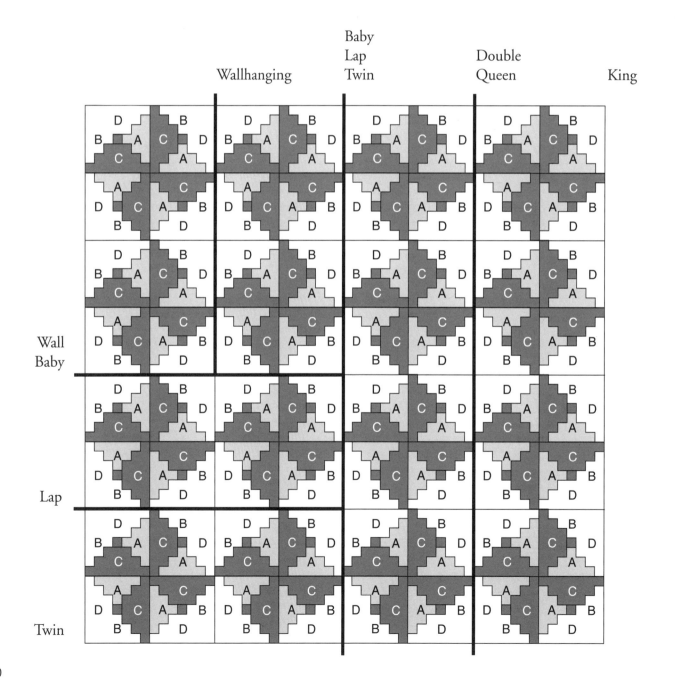

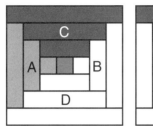 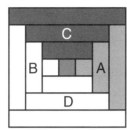

Block 4
Chevrons Layout

Start from center.

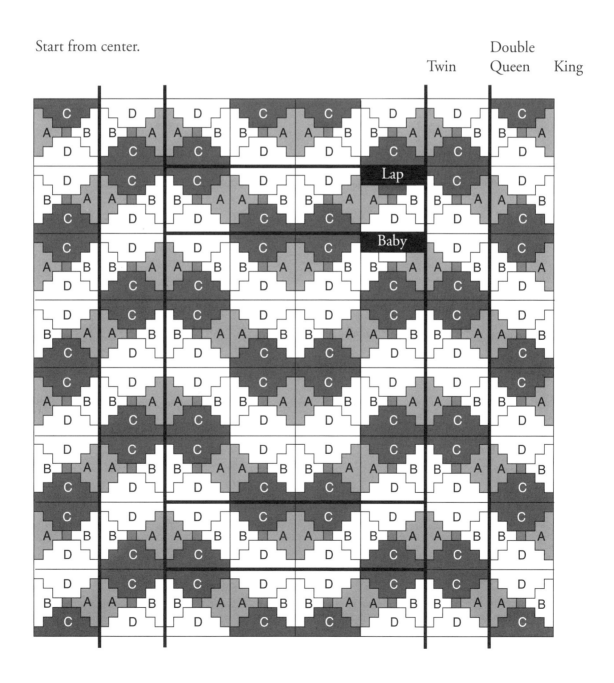

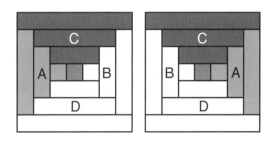

Block 4, Dark Center
Lanterns Barn Raising Layout

Start from center.

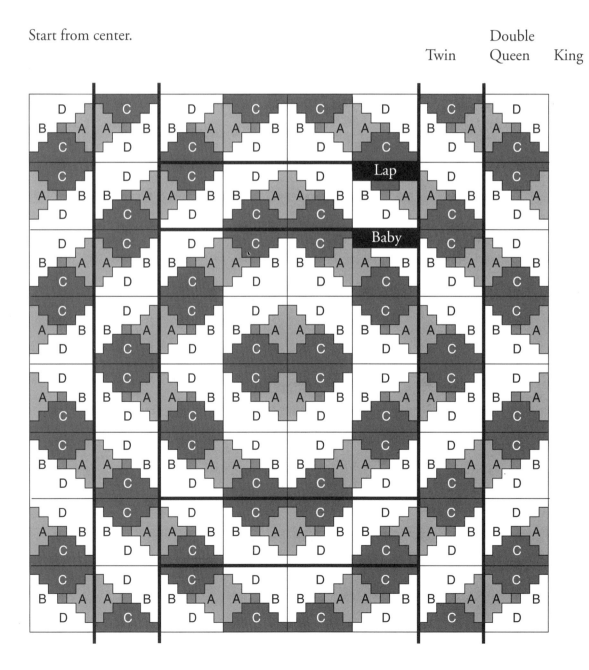

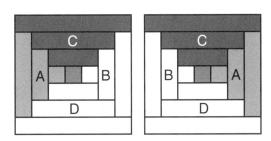

Block 4, Light Center

Lanterns Barn Raising Layout

Start from center.

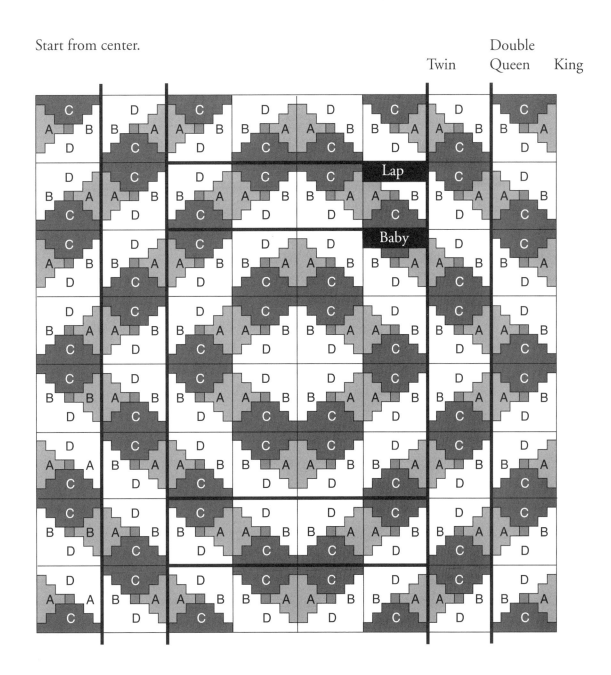

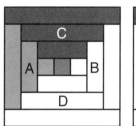 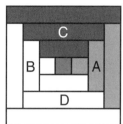

Block 4
Butterflies Layout

Start from center.

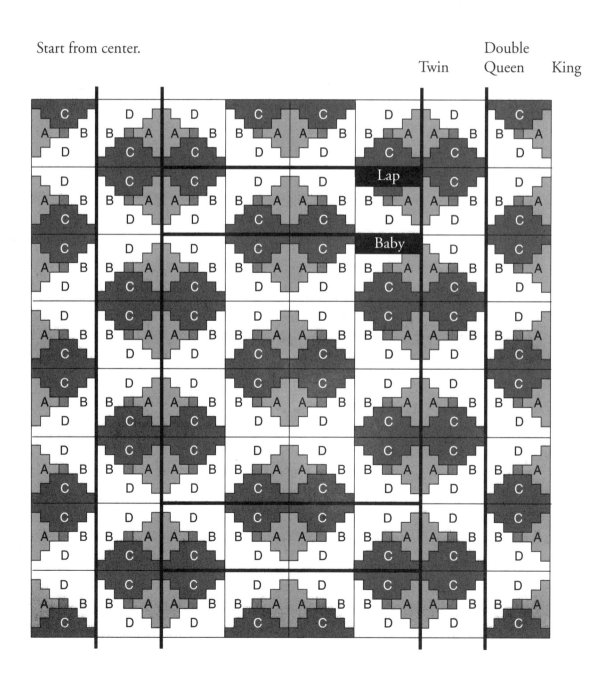

SEWING THE BLOCKS TOGETHER

Sewing the Vertical Rows in Pairs

1. Start with blocks in Rows 1 and 2. Flip blocks in Row 2 right sides together with blocks in Row 1.

2. Starting at top, stack block pair on blocks below. Stack these on pair below.

3. Repeat for all pairs, keeping first blocks on top.

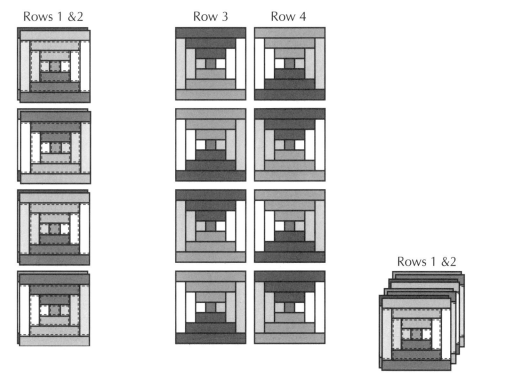

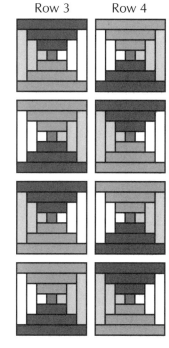

4. Lay paired blocks to right side of sewing machine.

5. Match the right sides of the paired blocks. Pin corners of blocks at both ends.

   Match and pin any seams that come together. Let seams lie in direction they were pressed.

6. Sew the length of the block, removing pins as you reach them. Do not cut threads.

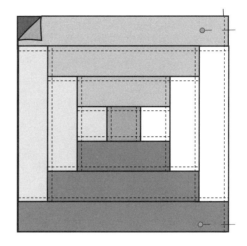

7. Pin and sew next blocks. Repeat for all stacked block pairs.

8. Remove from machine, but do not cut threads connecting blocks. Open blocks.

Check to make sure blocks are turned as in your choice of layout.

9. Flip top pair down onto second pair, pin and sew horizontal seam, pushing vertical seams in opposite directions every other block.

10. Repeat flipping sewn pairs down onto next pair until all horizontal rows are sewn in Rows 1 and 2.

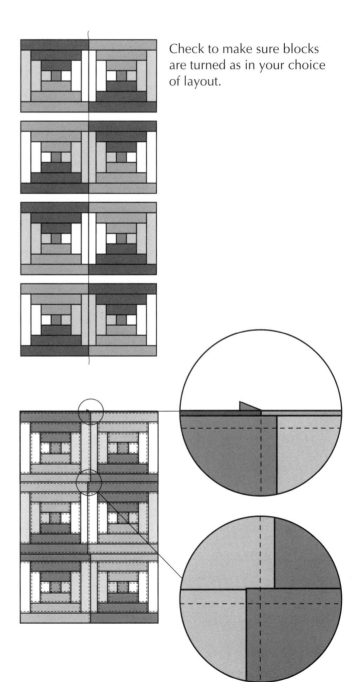

11. Repeat with Rows 3 and 4. Repeat for quilts with Rows 5 and 6, and 7 and 8.

12. Press as seams lie on each section.

13. Sew sections together.

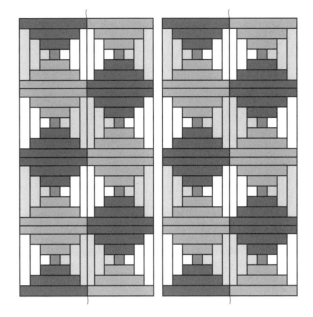

14. Press vertical seams before adding borders.

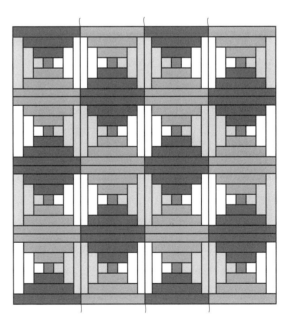

Be creative when adding borders. Suggested border yardage and border examples are given for each quilt. However, you may wish to custom design the borders by changing the widths of the strips. This might change backing yardage.

When custom fitting the quilt, lay the top on your bed before adding the borders and backing. Measure to find how much border is needed to get the fit you want. Keep in mind that the quilt will shrink approximately 3" in the length and width after tying, stitching in the ditch, and/or machine quilting.

ADDING THE BORDERS

Piecing Borders and Binding Strips

1. Stack and square off the ends of each strip, trimming away the selvage edges.

2. Seam the strips of each fabric into long pieces by assembly-line sewing. Lay the first strip right side up. Lay the second strip right sides to it. Backstitch, stitch the short ends together, and backstitch again.

3. Take the strip on the top and fold it so the right side is up.

4. Place the third strip right sides to it, backstitch, stitch, and backstitch again.

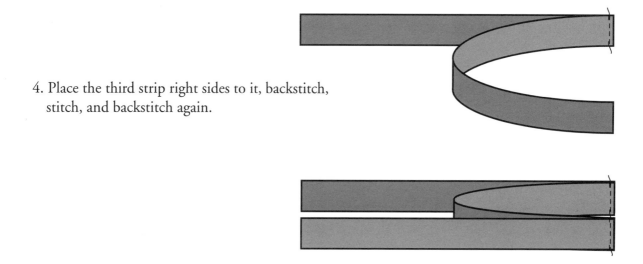

5. Continue assembly-line sewing all the short ends together into long pieces for each fabric.

6. Clip the threads holding the strips together.

7. Press seams to one side.

Sewing the Borders to the Quilt Top

1. Measure down the center to find the length. Cut two side strips that measurement plus two inches.

2. Right sides together, match and pin the center of the strips to the center of the sides. Pin at ends, allowing an extra inch of border at each end. Pin intermittently. Sew with the quilt on top. Set and direct the seams, pressing toward the borders.

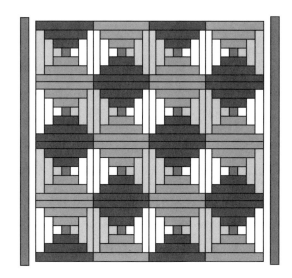

3. Square the ends even with the top and bottom of the quilt.

4. Measure the width across the center including newly added borders. Cut two strips that measurement plus two inches.

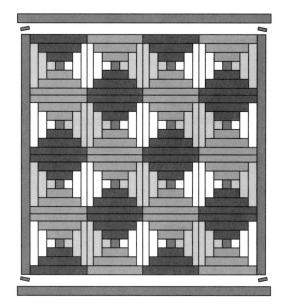

5. Right sides together, match and pin the center of the strips to the center of the top and bottom edges of the quilt. Pin at the ends, allowing an extra inch of border at both ends. Pin intermittently. Sew with the quilt on top.

6. Set and direct the seams, pressing toward the borders. Square the ends even with the side borders.

   Repeat these steps for additional borders.

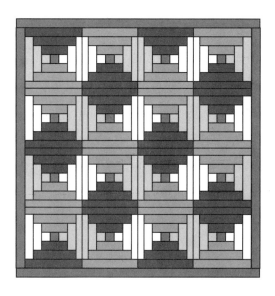

MACHINE QUILTING

Measuring the Quilt Top

Lay your quilt top on a flat surface. Measure length and width. Purchase a thin, bonded batting at least 5" wider and longer.

Layering the Quilt Top with Backing and Batting

1. Piece the backing yardage together for larger size quilts. Backing should be 5" larger than the quilt top.

2. Smooth out the backing right side down on a large floor area or table. Tape down on a floor area or clamp onto a table with large binder clips.

3. Place and smooth out the batting on top. Lay the quilt top right side up and centered on top of the batting. Completely smooth all layers until they are flat. Tape or clip securely. The backing and batting should extend at least 2" on all sides.

4. Decide if you want **Stairstep Machine Quilting** or **Straight Line Machine Quilting**.

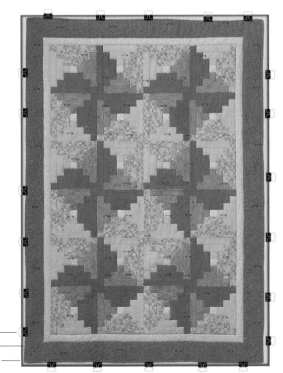

50

Stairstep Machine Quilting

You may choose to "stitch in the ditch" between colors. Decide where you want to stitch. Allow room for the walking foot when safety pinning near these seams.

Straight Line Machine Quilting

Decide where you want the quilting lines. With the 6" x 24" ruler, lightly mark the lines for machine quilting. Use chalk, a thin dry sliver of soap, a hera tool, or a silver pencil. Make certain that you can remove the marks from the fabric.

Diagonal Stairstep Quilting

Off Point Quilting

Horizontal Stairstep Quilting

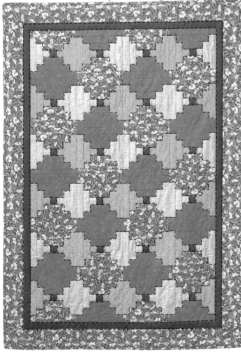

Continuous Diagonal Quilting

Quick and Easy Safety Pinning

Place 1" safety pins throughout the quilt away from the marked quilting lines. Or if you are stairstep quilting, pin on either side of the seam line. Begin pinning in the center and work to the outside, spacing them every 5". Grasp the opened pin in your right hand and the pinning tool in your left hand. Push the pin through the three layers, and bring the tip of the pin back out. Catch the tip in the groove of the tool and allow point to extend far enough to push pin closure down.

Machine Quilting

Use a walking foot attachment. Use invisible thread in the top of your machine and regular thread in the bobbin to match the backing. Loosen the top tension, and lengthen your stitch to 8 - 10 stitches per inch, or a #3 or #4 setting. Free arm machines need the bed placed for more surface area.

Walking Foot

1. Trim the backing and batting to within 2" of the outside edge of the quilt.

2. Roll the quilt tightly from the outside edge in toward middle. Hold this roll with quilt clips.

Jaws™

3. Slide this roll into the keyhole of the sewing machine.

4. Place the needle in the depth of the seam and pull up the bobbin thread. Lock the beginning and ending of each quilting line by backstitching.

5. Place your hands flat on both sides of the needle to form a hoop. Keep the quilt area flat and tight. If you need to ease in the top fabric, feed the quilt through the machine by pushing the layers of fabric and batting forward underneath the walking foot.

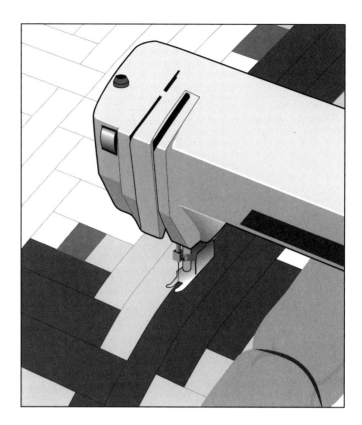

6. If puckering occurs, remove stitching by grasping the bobbin thread with a pin or tweezers and pull gently to expose the invisible thread. Touch the invisible thread stitches with the rotary cutter blade as you pull the bobbin thread free from the quilt.

7. Unroll, roll, and machine quilt, sewing the length or width or diagonal of the quilt.

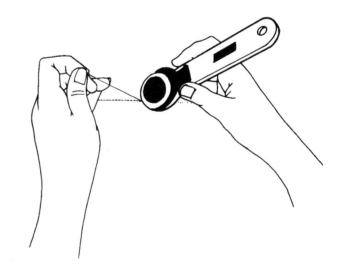

BINDING

Adding the Binding

Piece the binding strips into one long strip.

Use a walking foot attachment and regular thread on top and in the bobbin to match the binding. Use 10 stitches per inch, or #3 setting.

1. Press the binding strip in half lengthwise with right sides out.

2. Line up the raw edges of the folded binding with the raw edge of the quilt top at the middle of one side.

3. Begin sewing 4" from the end of the binding.

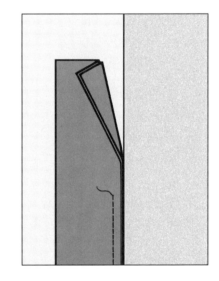

4. At the corner, stop the stitching ¼" from the edge with the needle in the fabric. Raise the presser foot and turn the quilt to the next side. Put the foot back down.

5. Sew backwards ¼" to the edge of the binding, raise the foot, and pull the quilt forward slightly.

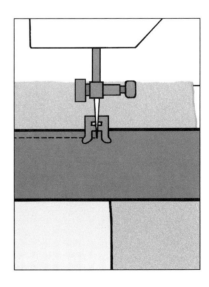

6. Fold the binding strip straight up on the diagonal. Fingerpress in the diagonal fold.

7. Fold the binding strip straight down with the diagonal fold underneath. Line up the top of the fold with the raw edge of the binding underneath.

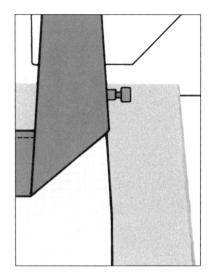

8. Fold the binding strip straight down with the diagonal fold underneath. Line up the top of the fold with the raw edge of the binding underneath.

9. Begin sewing from the corner.

10. Continue sewing and mitering the corners around the outside of the quilt.

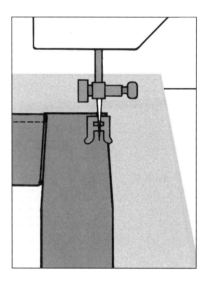

11. Stop sewing 4" from where the ends will overlap.

12. Line up the two ends of binding. Trim the excess with a ½" overlap.

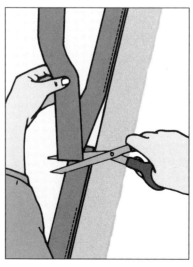

13. Open out the folded ends and pin right sides together. Sew a ¼" seam.

14. Continue to sew the binding in place.

15. Trim the batting and backing to ¼" from the binding.

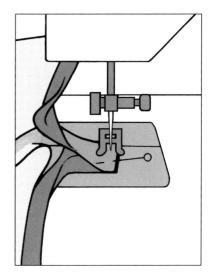

16. Fold the binding to the backside of the quilt. Pin in place so that the folded edge on the binding covers the stitching line. Tuck in the excess fabric at each miter on the diagonal.

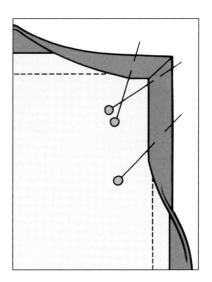

17. From the right side, "stitch in the ditch" using invisible thread on the right side, and a bobbin thread to match the binding on the back side. Catch the folded edge of the binding on the back side with the stitching.

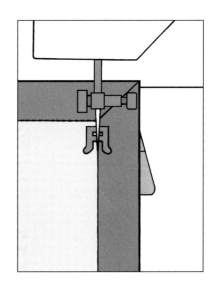

COURTHOUSE STEPS FROM SCRAPS

Scrap 1

It is possible to make a scrap Courthouse Steps quilt with a traditional look. This quilt is easy to sew following the instructions. Many different fabrics are used to create the scrappy look.

Planning the Quilt

Refer to Block 1 yardage chart. Gather the equivalent number of two inch wide strips specified for your size quilt. Use partial strips, as well as full length strips.

To clearly define the design it is important to divide the strips into three catagories:

Light Backgrounds Ecru and whites with small florals are used excusively on the A side of the block.

Pastels Soft pastel fabrics appear on the B side.

Darks Darkest floral and bright fabrics share the C and D side.

Center Square A wide range of medium and dark fabrics are used.

Follow Block 1 to sew your quilt. Use the Lanterns layout to put the quilt together.

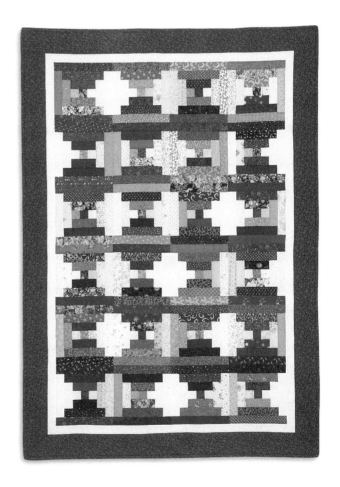

Scrap Quilt 2

This scrap quilt is more challenging to plan and sew. Do not attempt to sew one until you have made the blocks following the instructions and are thoroughly familiar with the construction steps.

Planning the Quilt

Refer to Block 1 yardage chart. You will need the equivalent number of two inch wide strips specified for your size quilt in a wide range of patterns and colors. Use multi-colored florals and fabrics that read as solid. Cut the strips from left over fabric from other projects. Use the partial strips saved from sewing your Courthouse Steps blocks for the center squares.

Use 2" wide strips.

You will need: • Large Lanterns, two strips
• Small Lanterns, one strip
• Half Lanterns at the edge of the quilt, one strip
• Center Piece 2" x 3"

Planning the First Four Blocks

Allow for a three foot square work space that can easily be seen from your sewing machine for laying out strips and planning your blocks. As the number of blocks increases you will need additional space.

Plan color placement for four blocks at a time.

1. Choose twelve contrasting fabrics. Refer to illustration for number of strips. Lay out squares.

2. Choose and lay out the Center pieces.

Strips represent boxed area in quilt above.

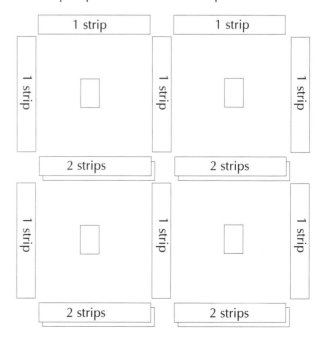

Making the Four Blocks

Making the "Left and Right Side" Strips

1. Measure and cut the Center piece 2" x 3" if it is not already that length.

2. Measure and cut the Left Side and Right Side strips 2" x 3". Lay out by matching partial strip. Do not cut the Middle strips.

3. Start at top left block. Flip the Center piece strip right sides together with the 2" x 3" strip nearest it. Repeat with Center piece and 2" x 3" strip on top right block.

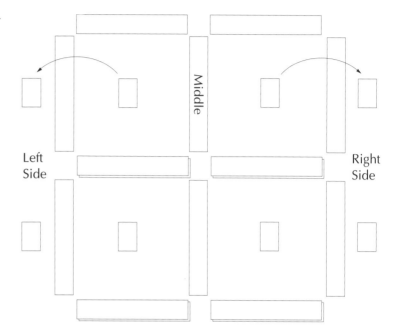

4. Sew length of both strips.

5. Lay on ironing board with Center piece on bottom. Lightly press closed block. Open strip and press.

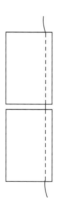

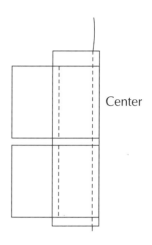

6. Pick up Middle strip.

7. Sew to opposite side of both Center pieces. Cut excess middle strip and return strip to position of blocks.

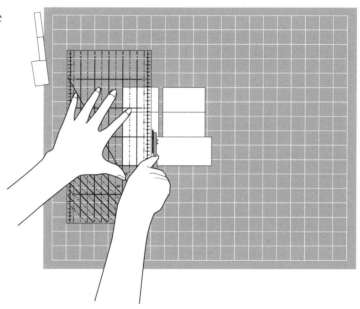

8. Lay sewn pairs on ironing board with strip side on top. Set seam and press strip open.

9. Lay on cutting mat. Square and cut 2" wide block.

10. Repeat for remaining two blocks.

Adding the Top and Bottom Strips

1. Lay blocks in center.

2. Start at top left block. Lay Top strip under presser foot. Lay sewn piece on strip with Middle fabric first.

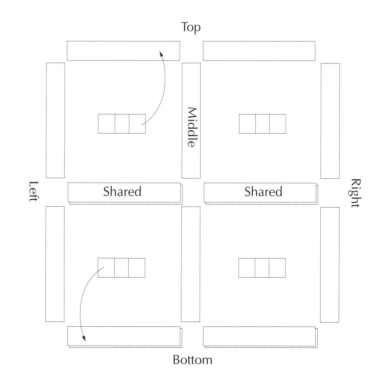

60

3. Sew length of block.

4. Use scissors to cut strip one inch beyond block and return strip to block layout.

5. Lay Bottom strip under presser foot. Lay sewn piece on strip with Left side fabric first.

6. Sew length of block.

7. Use scissors to cut strip one inch beyond block and return to block layout.

8. Lay on ironing board with strip side on top. Set seam and press strip open.

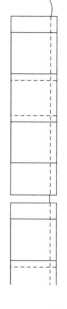

9. Add both blocks to Shared strip.

10. Lay on ironing board with strip side on top. Press and open strip.

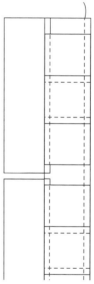

11. Lay on cutting mat. Line horizontal line of ruler on seam line and edge of ruler along side of block. Square blocks.

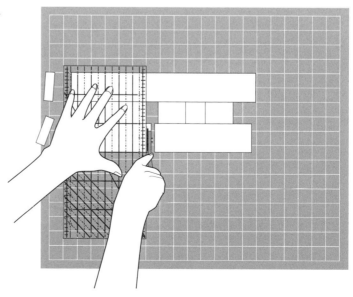

12. Lay out in center of block for placement. Double check that all sides are added correctly.

13. Stack strips and arrange by right side of sewing machine.

14. Stack blocks. Assembly-line sew four blocks, matching block to strip each time. The blocks are complete when three strips are added beyond the Center Square.

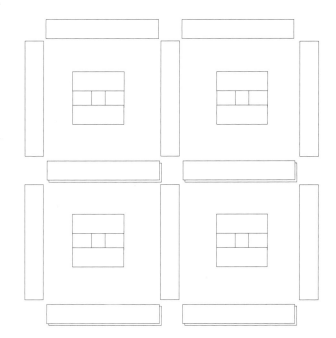

15. Lay out completed blocks.

16. Lay out partial strips by matching block side. Plan next four blocks. Repeat.

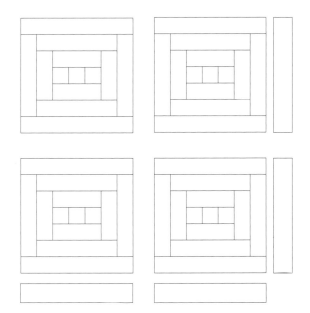

INDEX

ACKNOWLEDGEMENTS

Special thanks to…

My sister, Eleanor, who helped me finally get on the right track when I was searching for the right look for my quilt.

Dia Butterfield for inspiring me to see the many color possibilities in the Courthouse Steps block.

Darlene Palmer who showed me a block variation I never would have thought of.

Teresa Varnes for asking me how to turn a Courthouse Steps into a Barn Raising and inspiring two new block variations.

All my students, who tested the book and helped me improve it with their comments, confusions, and questions.

Bliss Berniece Bilbrey Sells for the use of her precious family Bible.

Mardi Snow at the San Diego Museum of Art for the use of their staircase.

Barbara Roldan and Annie Fallon, who filled me with joy, when they got as excited as I did and made quilt after quilt, trying all the variations.

Lindsay, Jill, and Dave King for the use of their quilt. Dave, thanks for carrying out my books.

And a very special thanks to Loretta Smith, for her unfailing support, inspiration and wizardry on the computer.

Quilt in a Day books offer a wide range of techniques and are directed toward a variety of skill levels. If you do not have a quilt shop in your area, you may write for a complete catalog and current price list of all books and patterns published by Quilt in a Day®, Inc.

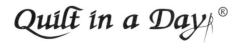

Quilt in a Day®, Inc. • 1955 Diamond Street, • San Marcos, CA 92069
1 800 777-4852 • Fax: (760) 591-4424 • www.quiltinaday.com